Debt
IN
AMERICA

By Edward Bradley

TABLE OF CONTENT

INTRODUCTION TO DEBT.. 3

THE DIFFERENT TYPES OF DEBT 5

THE REASON FOR BEING IN DEBT..8

BANKRUPTCY..13

HOW TO AVOID BANKRUPTCY..19

HOW TO GET OUT OF DEBT.. 21

 DEBT CONSOLIDATION..23

 HOW DOES DEBT CONSOLIDATION WORK...................................25

PROS AND CONS OF CONSOLIDATION..27

 RISKS OF DEBT CONSOLIDATION...31

REQUIREMENTSFORDEBTCONSOLIDATION...................................31

DEBT CONSOLIDATION AND CREDIT SCORES................................32

EFFECTIVE DEBT CONSOLIDATION PAYMENT STRATEGY................33

 DRAWBACKS OF DEBT CONSOLIDATION......................................34

HOW TO DECIDE TO CONSOLIDATE YOUR DEBT..............................39

HOW TO GET A DEBT CONSOLIDATION LOAN...............................40

WHEN YOU SHOULD CONSOLIDATE YOUR DEBT...........................43

BUDGET AND FINANCIAL STABILITY..44

IMPORTANCE OF MANAGING DEBT...47

HOW TO ENCOURAGE PEOPLE IN DEBT..50

INTRODUCTION TO DEBT

Debt is common among most people because it provides short-term funds for long-term assets. While debt is sometimes viewed as a necessary evil, having too much of it can be detrimental to your financial health. This article will explain what debt is, how it works, and how to manage it safely. Discuss the various types of debt and the potential pitfalls of over-indebtedness. So, if you want to better understand debt and how it affects your finances, keep reading! You can keep your financial health in check by understanding the basic principles of debt and taking steps to deal with it responsibly.

First, let's go over the fundamentals of debt and its various forms, so you can better understand how it works. Then go over how to effectively manage debt and avoid taking on too much. Finally, discuss strategies for debt reduction and long-term success.

The most common forms of debt are loans, including mortgages, auto loans, personal loans, and credit card debt. Under the terms of a loan, the borrower is required to repay the balance of the loan by a certain date, typically several years in the future. The terms of the loan also stipulate the amount of interest that the borrower is required to pay annually, expressed as a percentage of the loan amount. Interest is used to ensure that the lender is compensated for taking on the risk of the loan while also encouraging the borrower to repay the loan quickly to limit their total interest expense.

WHAT IS DEBT

A debt is an agreement in which one person, organization, or country owes money to another. A government may owe another government, an individual to a bank or other financial institution, or a corporation to its shareholders. Debts are sums of money that are owed or that must be paid. It is a liability incurred by a natural or legal person as a result of borrowing money or taking out a loan.

Bank loans, credit cards, and personal loans are all examples of debt sources. Liability is another term for debt. Debt occurs when one party lends money to another, and the borrower is required to repay the loan plus interest. **Debt also refers to the obligation to repay a loan as well as any interest owed on the loan.**

THE DIFFERENT TYPES OF DEBT

There are numerous types of debt, each with its own set of terms, conditions, and repayment options. Here are a few examples of the most common types of debt:

- **SECURED DEBT**

To secure the loan, the borrower must put up collateral, such as a tangible asset or property. Furthermore, the lender is required to return the borrowed funds on a mutually agreed-upon date. Before granting the loan, the bank evaluates the borrower's creditworthiness and ability to repay. If the borrower fails to make monthly payments, the creditor has the right to seize or sell the asset or property in question to recover the debt. Automobile, mortgage, and credit card loans are common examples

- **MORTGAGE DEBT:**

A mortgage is a loan that is used to buy a home. Because the home serves as collateral for the loan, if you default on the loan, the lender may foreclose on your home. Mortgage debt typically has a longer repayment term and a lower interest rate than other types of debt, such as credit card debt.

- **AUTOMOBILE DEBT:**

Auto loans are used to finance the acquisition of a vehicle. Auto loan debt is typically secured by the vehicle itself, which means that if you default on your loan, the lender has the right to repossess the vehicle.

UNSECURED DEBT

It does not require the borrower to secure the loan with the collateral. Hence, the lender may face difficulty retrieving the money if the borrower defaults. That is why the lender considers the creditworthiness and repayment potential of the borrower when issuing the loan. Furthermore, the interest rates are usually higher in unsecured loans than in any other loan form. If the borrower fails to repay the loan, the lender may file a lawsuit against them to cover the losses. Common examples include credit card bills, medical costs, student loans, payday loans, etc.

- **MEDICAL DEBT:**

Medical debt is debt incurred for medical expenses. This type of debt can be especially difficult to pay off due to the high cost of healthcare and the fact that many people are unable to work while they are recovering from an illness or injury

- **STUDENT LOAN DEBT:**

Student loans are loans used to finance education costs. Like mortgage debt, student loan debt typically has a longer repayment term and lower interest rate than other types of debt. However, unlike mortgage debt, student loan debt is not secured by any collateral. This means that if you default on your student loans, the lender cannot take your home or any other property as compensation.

- **REVOLVING DEBT**

This is a loan cycle in which the borrower can borrow up to a certain credit limit as long as they continue to make small payments to the creditor. Furthermore, it allows the borrower to borrow money and repay the balance at their leisure and convenience. Furthermore, the amount lent changes over time. Some examples are credit cards, store cards, and credit accounts at local grocery stores.

- **CREDIT CARD DEBT:**

Unsecured debt that is typically used for purchases or cash advances referred to as "credit card debt." Credit cards, on average, have higher interest rates and shorter repayment terms than other types of loans. This type of debt is particularly difficult to repay if you only make minimum monthly payments, which frequently only cover the interest on the outstanding balance.

NON-REVOLVING/INSTALLMENT DEBT

It is a one-time credit option in which the borrower borrows a specific amount of money for a specific period and repays it in monthly installments. As a result, it takes a long time to clear completely. It, like all loans, has a high-interest rate. As a result, the borrower pays a significant amount in comparison to the amount borrowed. **Examples include student and home loans.**

CORPORATE DEBT

Corporations, like individuals, may seek funds to further their business-related activities. These are referred to as "corporate loans." Businesses raise capital by issuing bonds or notes to investors with the promise of repayment. Firms must, however, refund the amount to bondholders at a predetermined maturity date in addition to regular fixed interests or coupons.

SNEAKY DEBT:

It is the most common type of loan used by middle-class families to furnish their homes. The infamous 0% interest rate may be used to finance almost anything, including furniture, home appliances, and cell phones. While it appears to be an appealing offer, it should be avoided at all costs.

THE REASON FOR BEING IN DEBT

- **LOW EARNINGS OR UNDEREMPLOYMENT:**

Because there isn't much money left over at the end of the month, some people with lower-paying jobs may struggle to meet their bills or save money. If you live paycheck to paycheck, you may find yourself in a bind if you receive a large bill or an unexpected payment.

- **DIVORCE AND RELATIONSHIP BREAKDOWN:**

As a couple, you become accustomed to having two incomes. However, your income could be cut in half or drastically reduced if you divorce. You may also have to deal with the significant expense of legal fees or regular payments to your ex-partner.

- **POOR MONEY MANAGEMENT:**

Manage your debts before they manage you. Examine your bank statements and keep a spending diary to determine what you're spending your money on and how far your income goes toward covering your outgoings. If you find yourself overspending, consider cutting back on your spending or calculating any savings you could make by switching your energy bills, phone contract, or even your mortgage.

- **HIGH LIVING EXPENSES**:

Some parts of the country have higher living costs than others. Higher house prices, rental demands, and longer commutes can all contribute to a higher cost of living. **All these factors affect regular expenses,** which could leave you short when it comes to meeting other financial obligations.

- **OVERUSE OF CREDIT CARDS:**

Store cards and interest-free credit deals may sound appealing, but if you can't keep up with repayments or are already in debt, it's best to avoid taking on any more. Talk to your credit card companies about a debt management plan and seek advice from organizations such as Citizens' Advice on the best way to consolidate credit card debt. It's also a good idea to avoid using credit cards exclusively. Although a credit card can provide payment protection and an improved credit rating in some cases unless you're confident in your ability to pay your credit card bills on time, try to stick to cash or debit transactions for the majority of your spending. If you have several credit cards, you could look into consolidating your debt to better manage your repayment plan.

- **UNEXPECTED EXPENSES:**

Accidents happen, whether it's the boiler breaking down or an illness that prevents you from working. When faced with large one-time payments, having access to savings or a good insurance policy can act as a buffer. These events are sometimes unavoidable and simply the result of bad luck, so having access to a fund to cover such emergencies is beneficial.

- **LOWERING HEALTH AND MEDICAL EXPENSES:**

Healthcare can be costly, from purchasing medication to ongoing costs if an illness prevents you from working. Many people are in debt because of declining health and medical expenses. Although living a healthy lifestyle is preferable, some illnesses are the result of unfortunate events or accidents. If you are facing spiraling medical costs, you should contact a debt relief charity or the relevant benefits department to see if you can get assistance with your medical expenses and health care.

- **JOB LOSS:**

A regular salary from a job provides a lot of security and ensures that you have enough money to pay your bills and put food on the table. If you lose your job or are unable to pay your bills, you may be faced with looming payments or be forced to use credit or debit services to cover your costs. Savings or a good insurance policy can come in handy in these situations. If you are unable to save, it is worth investigating whether you are eligible for government assistance in the form of benefits.

- **EDUCATION AND STUDENT DEBT:**

This is a common type of debt, particularly among young people. Going to university or continuing your education with a master's program can be a great way to help you achieve your goals and advance in your chosen career. However, both undergraduate and postgraduate education is costly, particularly in the United Kingdom. Debt repayments work differently than other types of debt, with a small portion of what you owe deducted from your wages when you do start working. Unlike some other types of debt, student loan debt is unlikely to harm your credit score.

- **LIVING BEYOND YOUR MEANS:**

Spending more money than you earn is the quickest way to get into debt. Even if it is not always possible, try to live within your means. Cutting unnecessary expenses and finding ways to reduce your monthly outgoings, such as traveling by foot or bike or cooking at home, can help you save money. You could always save the money or use it to pay off existing debt faster.

- **LACK OF A BUDGET:**

One of the most basic causes of debt is a lack of a budget. You may be more likely to spend more than you have access to if you are unaware of how much money you have. You can stay on top of payments and be more aware of how much money is left in your account if you monitor your finances. A monthly budget can help you cover bills and other important expenses first, as well as give you an idea of how much extra money you have each month.

- **LACK OF AN EMERGENCY FUND OR SAVINGS:**

Saving money can be difficult, especially if you are already in debt or your monthly pay packet does not allow for wiggle room. However, by setting aside a small emergency fund, or even enough to cover a few months' expenses, you can put yourself in a good position if something goes wrong. With an emergency fund, you could cover some emergency expenses without taking out a loan, or you could cover yourself for a few months if you lost your job.

- **HAVING CHILDREN:**

For many people, having children is a wonderful experience and a life goal. Having children, on the other hand, is not cheap. There are numerous additional costs associated with having children, ranging from childcare to food, clothing, and toys. Some parents may be forced to incur additional debt to continue to provide for their children. In this case, you should contact a debt relief organization or apply for additional benefit.

- **FAILED BUSINESSES AND BUSINESS EXPENSES:**

Starting your own business can be both rewarding and profitable. Many businesses, however, fail and go bankrupt. You will be personally liable for any debts incurred by the company as its owner. Starting a business can be costly, and some entrepreneurs take on debt or a bank loan to get things started in the hope that their business will be profitable enough in the future to repay the loan. This is not always the case, and if your business fails, you will still owe the bank the money you borrowed for start-up costs.

BANKRUPTCY

Inability to pay your debts, or a specific example of this involving the sale of your property or some other arrangement to pay as much of the money you owe as possible.

Bankruptcy is a legal procedure that allows individuals or businesses to be free of their debts while also providing creditors with an opportunity for repayment.

Bankruptcy is handled in federal courts, and the rules are laid out in the United States Bankruptcy Code.

There are various types of bankruptcy, which are commonly referred to by their chapter in the United States Bankruptcy Code.

For example, Chapter 11 bankruptcy allows businesses to reorganize and reemerge, whereas Chapter 7 bankruptcy is for individuals.

Bankruptcy can provide you with a fresh start, but it will remain on your credit reports for several years and make future borrowing difficult.

There are six (6) types of bankruptcy

1. **CHAPTER 7**

    When a business has no chance of survival, Chapter 7 bankruptcy is usually the last resort. This is also referred to as liquidation. When a company's debts cannot be restructured, it usually files for Chapter 7. Furthermore, a debtor who is about to file for this type of bankruptcy usually lacks substantial assets.

    If the effort required to reorganize the company exceeds the owner's capabilities, Chapter 7 is a viable option. A court-appointed trustee will be in charge of canceling the company's debts by selling assets and distributing the proceeds to creditors in this bankruptcy form.

After all, debts have been paid, a sole proprietor is usually discharged, which means that he or she is no longer liable for their debts. A corporation or partnership that files for Chapter 7 bankruptcy cannot be discharged. It is important to note, however, that not all debts can be discharged, and a lien on the property is not canceled after the discharge.

Chapter 7 bankruptcy is the most common type of bankruptcy, among people who have the opportunity to start over after failing. This chapter is the most convenient solution when the debtor has no way of repaying the money owed, there are no cosigners, and legal action by creditors is imminent. Individuals go through a similar process; their nonexempt assets are collected and converted to cash, and the proceeds are divided among creditors by the provisions of the Bankruptcy Code. Typically, the debtor will be discharged at the end of the procedure and will no longer be personally liable for the remaining dischargeable debts.

2. CHAPTER 11

When there is still hope of getting the business back on track, Chapter 11 bankruptcy is usually preferred over other types of bankruptcy. The goal of this chapter is to assist the company in recovering through reorganization.

During the bankruptcy process, Chapter 11 ensures business continuity. The court may appoint a trustee under this chapter. However, most of the time, the business owner is permitted to continue operating as a debtor in possession (DIP). This bankruptcy form is carried out by the debtor's reorganization plan. The company describes how it intends to repay its creditors in this plan. If trustee committees are appointed, they will represent the creditors' interests and assist the debtor in developing the plan. The plan will be reviewed by the creditors, who must vote on it. To be the plan must also be approved by the court. This process may take some time; companies may have to wait for more than a year to receive approval.

After the plan is approved, the debtor can begin reorganizing the business by retaining its essential assets and paying creditors from the profits generated. Even if the reorganization plan is approved by the court and the debtor continues to manage his or her company, any major business decision they wish to implement will also require court approval. This chapter is typically chosen by large corporations. Small businesses avoid it because it is too expensive to obtain plan approval. Furthermore, the process can take anywhere between 6 months and 2 years to complete.

Companies that complete a Chapter 11 bankruptcy typically benefit from reduced debts and newly organized business. While Chapter 11 is most commonly used by businesses, it is also available to individuals.

3. **CHAPTER 13**

This bankruptcy chapter provides consumers with a reorganization form. This option assists people with a steady income in repaying their debts. A repayment plan, which the debtor must file and the court must approve, governs Chapter 13 bankruptcy. This plan outlines the steps that the debtor will take to repay his or her debts. The amount of money that debtors must repay varies according to their income, debts, and property. Debtors have 3 to 5 years to repay their debts under this chapter. After the court approves the plan, the debtor begins paying creditors through a trustee. Once the approval is obtained, the creditor is granted protection, and creditors will be unable to sue him or her. The debtor is discharged of the remaining debt once the plan is completed. For those who own a sole proprietorship, Chapter 13 is also an option. Among the benefits of Chapter 13 are:

- The debtor's ability to save their house from foreclosure
- The possibility to reschedule and extend secured debts
- The protection granted to third parties, like co-signers, who are responsible for consumer debts
- The lack of direct contact between debtor and creditors; debtors send the payments to the trustee who then pays the creditors
- When a debtor has debts that cannot be discharged under Chapter 7, such as taxes or child support, or liens that exceed the value of their assets, Chapter 13 can help. This type of bankruptcy is also appropriate when debtors fail to file their taxes or cover their house expenses for an extended period.

4. CHAPTER 12

Chapter 12 is a unique type of bankruptcy; it is only available to businesses engaged in agriculture or fishing. This chapter enables family businesses that operate in these sectors to restructure their operations and avoid liquidation. Chapter 12 works in the same way that Chapter 13 does. This chapter has the following advantages:

- Most companies can continue their business operations after they've filed for Chapter 12
- Although a trustee is appointed, their duties are restricted; checking documents, monitoring operations, planning payments collection and disbursement
- companies filing for this chapter have 90 days to come forward with a repayment plan and the deadline can sometimes be extended
- the debtor gets 3 to 5 years to pay off his or her debts
- debtors can benefit from a cram down for their secured debts

5. **CHAPTER 9**

    Municipalities such as cities, towns, villages, counties, taxing districts, municipal utilities, or school districts that require reorganization may file for Chapter 9 bankruptcy. This chapter seeks to assist municipalities in financial distress and to protect them from creditors. The municipality filing for chapter 9 will devise and implement a plan to assist it in debt adjustment. Municipalities that attempt to restructure their debts typically use one of three approaches: extending debt maturities, obtaining a new loan to refinance the debt, or obtaining an interest reduction. Unlike other types of bankruptcy, Chapter 9 does not involve asset liquidation and distribution among creditors. Municipalities that are authorized to be debtors, insolvent, and willing to implement a debt adjustment plan may file for Chapter 9 bankruptcy.

6. **CHAPTER 15**

    Chapter 15 bankruptcy is a newer type of bankruptcy that has been available since 2005 and allows foreign debtors to file for bankruptcy under US laws. This chapter is essentially an adoption of the United Nations Commission on International Trade Law's international bankruptcy laws. Each year, only a few cases are filed under this chapter.

    Chapter 15 of the Bankruptcy Code has been added to ensure coordination for cross-border insolvencies and to provide a faster and more efficient method of resolving them. To begin this procedure, a petition for recognition of the foreign proceeding is filed by an appointed foreign representative. The foreign proceeding is recognized after the court hearing, and the representative can seek relief. You should consult with a bankruptcy attorney to fully understand the benefits and drawbacks of each bankruptcy chapter, as well as how they may affect your business or personal estate. Based on your requirements, an expert will assist you in selecting the most appropriate procedure.

HOW TO AVOID BANKRUPTCY

MAINTAINING A CASH-FLOW BALANCE.

Cash flow management assists you in determining how much money your company requires to cover debts, such as paying employees and suppliers.

- Don't wait to send invoices
- Adjust your inventory as needed
- Lease your equipment instead of buying it
- Borrow money before you need it
- Reevaluate your business operations
- Restructure your payments and collections
- Monitor where your money is going
- Take advantage of technology

MAKING DECISIONS BASED ON A BUSINESS PLAN.

- Executive Summary
- Company Description
- Products and Services
- Market analysis
- Strategy and Implementation
- Organization and Management Team
- Financial plan and projections

KEEPING ACCURATE FINANCIAL REPORTS.

- Establish Business Bank Accounts
- Avoid Using Cash
- Schedule a Specific Time Each Week.
- Purchase the Right Accounting Software
- Tax Obligations
- Keep a Complete Record of Accounting Documents

- Invest in an Experienced Bookkeeper

MAINTAINING GOOD RELATIONSHIPS WITH CREDITORS.

- Negotiate payment terms with your suppliers
- Offer discounts for early repayment
- Change payment terms
- Automate credit control, and set up chasers
- External credit control
- Improve stock control

HOW TO GET OUT OF DEBT

1. PRIORITIZING YOUR DEBT REPAYMENTS

HOW TO PRIORITIZE YOUR DEBT:

- **PRIORITY PAYMENTS**:
  This means paying off the most important bills first, sometimes even before your debt. Keeping up with your mortgage, rent, and utility bills can help you avoid incurring additional debt.

- **PAY-OFF DEBTS**:
  Paying off your debts to businesses, banks, and loan providers is more important than eating out or going to the movies. Make a payment plan with your creditors to ensure that you can manage your debt repayments.

- **MAKE A BUDGET**:
  Knowing how much money you have and planning your monthly expenses can assist you in knowing where your money is going. You may also notice areas where you could potentially save money.

- **MONITOR YOUR CASH**:
  Keeping a close eye on your finances is important, so you can be aware of when bills are due and how much money you have in your account.

2. NEGOTIATING WITH CREDITOR

If you want to negotiate a lower monthly payment with your creditors, you'll need to demonstrate why you can't afford the current payments. They'll usually want to see a household budget that includes your income and essential living expenses to determine how much you can realistically afford.

3. **DEBT CONSOLIDATION**

    The act of taking out a new loan to pay off other liabilities and consumer debts is referred to as "debt consolidation." Multiple debts are consolidated into a single, larger debt with better payoff terms, such as a lower interest rate, a lower monthly payment, or both.

4. **DEBT MANAGEMENT PLAN**

    A debt management plan is an agreement between you and your creditors (the companies to whom you owe money) to make a fixed monthly payment. Companies known as "debt management plan operators" or "providers" manage the plans and negotiate with your creditors on your behalf.

- Step one: Sort out your priority debts.
- Step two: determine whether a DMP is right for you.
- Step three: determine your budget;
- Step four: consider whether to pay for your DMP
- Step five: select a DMP provider.

DEBT CONSOLIDATION

Debt consolidation is the act of taking out a new loan to pay off other liabilities and consumer debt. Multiple debts are combined into a single, larger debt with more favorable payoff terms, such as a lower interest rate, a lower monthly payment, or both.

TYPES OF DEBT CONSOLIDATION

You can consolidate debt by using various types of loans. The type of debt consolidation that is best for you will be determined by the terms and types of your current loans, as well as your current financial situation. Debt consolidation loans are classified into two types: Secured loans and Unsecured loans.

- Secured loans are backed by an asset, such as your home, which serves as collateral for the loan.
- Unsecured loans, on the other hand, are not backed by assets and can be more difficult to get. They also tend to have higher interest rates and lower qualifying amounts.

With either type of loan, interest rates are still typically lower than the rates charged on credit cards. And in most cases, the rates are **fixed**, so they do not vary over the repayment period

Here are some common ways to consolidate debt:

1. PERSONAL LOAN

It is an unsecured loan from a bank or credit union that provides a lump sum payment that can be used for any purpose. The loan is then repaid with regular monthly payments for a set period at a fixed interest rate. Personal loans typically have lower interest rates than credit cards, making them ideal for debt consolidation. However, if you use a personal loan to pay off credit cards, make sure you don't keep spending on them, or your debt problem will be exacerbated by the consolidation.

A debt consolidation loan is a personal loan designed specifically for debt consolidation. They are designed to help people who are struggling with multiple high-interest loans.

2. CREDIT CARD

If it has a lower interest rate and you stop using your old cards, a new card can help you reduce your credit card debt. Some credit cards offer a 0% APR introductory period that, if used correctly for balance transfers, can significantly reduce the total interest you pay on credit card debt. Be aware of the credit card's interest rate after the introductory period expires, and make sure you won't end up paying more in interest if you can't pay off the balance before then.

3. HOME EQUITY LOAN

A home equity loan or home equity line of credit (HELOC) can be a useful way to consolidate debt if you are a homeowner with equity. These secured loans use your equity as collateral and typically offer interest rates that are slightly higher than average mortgage rates but significantly lower than credit card interest rates.

4. STUDENT LOAN PROGRAM

For people with student loans, the federal government provides several consolidation options, including direct consolidation loans through the Federal Direct Loan Program. The new interest rate is calculated by taking the weighted average of the previous loans. Private loans, on the other hand, are not eligible for this program.

HOW DOES DEBT CONSOLIDATION WORKS

Debt consolidation is the process of repaying existing debts with new funds. If you have multiple types of debt, you can apply for a loan to combine them into a single liability and pay them off as a single loan. Payments are then made on the new debt until it is completely paid off.

Debt consolidation may result in a lower interest rate, lowering the overall cost of your debt. It can also reduce your monthly payment amount, making it easier to pay your bills. Finally, some people

consolidate debt to simplify their bills by paying only one lender rather than multiple lenders. And if you don't incur any new debt, you'll be able to pay off your debt faster.

You can roll old debt into new debt in a variety of ways, including with a new personal loan, credit card, or home equity loan. Then you use the new loan to pay off your smaller loans. You can make a credit card balance transfer from your original card to your new one if you are using a new credit card to consolidate other credit card debt. Creditors are frequently willing to collaborate with you on debt consolidation to increase the likelihood that you will repay your debt.

EXAMPLE OF DEBT CONSOLIDATION

For example, if you have three credit cards and owe a total of $20,000 with a 22.99% annual rate compounded monthly, you would need to pay $1,047.37 a month for 24 months to bring the balances down to zero. You will pay $5,136.88 in interest over time.

If you consolidated those credit cards into a lower-interest loan at an 11% annual rate compounded monthly, you would need to pay $932.16 a month for the same 24 months to pay off the debt, and you would pay a total of $2,371.84 in interest. Your monthly savings would be $115.21, and your total savings would be $2,765.04.

Consolidating three credit cards with an average interest rate of 22.99%		
Loan Details	Credit Cards (3)	Consolidation Loan
Principal	$20,000	$20,000
Interest %	22.99%	11%
Payments	$1,047.37	$932.16
Term	24 months	24 months
Bills Paid/Month	3	1
Total Interest	$5,136.88	$2,371.84

PROS AND CONS OF CONSOLIDATION

PROS OF DEBT CONSOLIDATION

Consolidating your debt can provide several benefits, including a faster, more streamlined payoff and lower interest payments.

1. **STREAMLINES FINANCES**

Combining multiple outstanding debts into a single loan reduces the number of payments and interest rates you must worry about. Consolidation can also help your credit by lowering your chances of missing or making a late payment. And, if you're working toward a debt-free lifestyle, you'll have a better idea of when all of your debt will be paid off.

2. **MAY EXPEDITE PAYOFF**

If the interest on your debt consolidation loan is lower than the interest on individual loans, consider making extra payments with the money you save each month. This can help you pay off the debt sooner, saving you even more money in interest in the long run. Keep in mind, however, that debt consolidation typically results in a longer loan term, so you'll need to make a point of paying off your debt as soon as possible to take advantage of this benefit.

3. **COULD LOWER INTEREST RATE**

Even if you have mostly low-interest loans and your credit score has improved since applying for other loans, you may be able to lower your overall interest rate by consolidating debts. This can save you money over the loan's life, especially if you don't consolidate with a long loan term. Shop around and focus on lenders that offer a personal loan pre qualification process to ensure you get the best rate possible.

However, keep in mind that some types of debt have higher interest rates than others. Credit cards, for example, typically have higher interest rates than student loans. Consolidating multiple debts with a single personal loan may result in a lower interest rate on some debts but a higher interest rate on others. In this case, concentrate on the total amount you're saving.

4. MAY REDUCE MONTHLY PAYMENT

Because future payments are spread out over a new and possibly extended loan term, your overall monthly payment is likely to decrease when you consolidate debt. While this can be advantageous in terms of monthly budgeting, it also means that you may pay more over the life of the loan, even if the interest rate is lower.

5. CAN IMPROVE CREDIT SCORE

Because of the hard credit inquiry, applying for a new loan may result in a temporary drop in your credit score. However, debt consolidation can help you improve your credit score in a variety of ways. Paying off revolving lines of credit, such as credit cards, can, for example, lower the credit utilization rate reflected in your credit report. Your utilization rate should ideally be less than 30%, and debt consolidation can help you get there. Making consistent, on-time payments and eventually paying off the loan can also help you improve your credit score over time.

CONS OF DEBT CONSOLIDATION

A debt consolidation loan or balance transfer credit card may seem like a good way to streamline debt payoff. That said, there are some risks and disadvantages associated with this strategy.

1. MAY COME WITH ADDED COSTS

Additional fees, such as origination fees, balance transfer fees, closing costs, and annual fees, may be incurred when obtaining a debt consolidation loan. Before signing on the dotted line with a lender, make sure you understand the true cost of each debt consolidation loan.

2. COULD RAISE YOUR INTEREST RATE

Debt consolidation can be a wise decision if you qualify for a lower interest rate. However, if your credit score isn't high enough to qualify for the best rates, you might be stuck with a rate that's higher than the one on your current debts. This could imply paying origination fees as well as more interest over the life of the loan.

1. YOU MAY PAY MORE IN INTEREST OVER TIME

Even if your interest rate falls when you consolidate, you may end up paying more in interest over the life of the new loan. When you consolidate debt, the repayment period begins on the first day and can last up to seven years. Although your overall monthly payment will be lower, interest will accrue for a longer period. To avoid this problem, plan for monthly payments that are greater than the minimum loan payment. This way, you can reap the benefits of a debt consolidation loan without incurring additional interest.

2. YOU RISK MISSING PAYMENTS

Missing payments on a debt consolidation loan, or any loan, can harm your credit score and subject you to additional fees. To avoid this, go over your budget and make sure you have enough money to cover the new payment. Once you've consolidated your debts, use autopay or any other tools that can help you avoid late payments. Also, if you believe you will miss an upcoming payment, notify your lender as soon as possible.

3. DOESN'T SOLVE UNDERLYING FINANCIAL ISSUES

Consolidating debt can make payments easier, but it does not address the underlying financial habits that led to the debts in the first place. Many borrowers who use debt consolidation end up in deeper debt because they did not limit their spending and continued to accumulate debt. So, if you're thinking about debt consolidation to pay off multiple maxed-out credit cards, start by developing good financial habits.

4. MAY ENCOURAGE INCREASED SPENDING

Similarly, paying off credit cards and other lines of credit with a debt consolidation loan may give the impression that you have more money than you do. Borrowers can easily fall into the trap of paying off debts only to discover that their balances have risen once more. Create a budget to help you cut back on spending and stay on top of payments so you don't end up in more debt than you started with.

RISKS OF DEBT CONSOLIDATION

Debt consolidation can provide several financial benefits, but there are some drawbacks to consider. For one thing, when you take out a new loan, your credit score may suffer a minor setback, which may affect your ability to qualify for other new loans. You may also end up paying more in total interest, depending on how you consolidate your loans. For example, if you obtain a new loan with lower monthly payments but a longer repayment term and a higher interest rate, you will almost certainly pay more total interest.

Check that the consolidation process saves you money and that the upfront costs of debt consolidation services do not interfere with your ability to make timely payments. Debt consolidation services frequently charge exorbitant upfront and monthly fees. Consider debt consolidation on your own with a bank personal loan or a low-interest credit card.

REQUIREMENTS FOR DEBT CONSOLIDATION

To qualify for a new loan, borrowers must meet the lender's income and creditworthiness requirements. Although the type of documentation you'll need is frequently determined by your credit history, For example, you may be required to provide a letter of employment, two months' worth of statements for each credit card or loan you wish to pay off, and letters from creditors or repayment agencies when applying for a debt consolidation loan.

When you receive your debt consolidation loan, decide which loans you will pay off first. In some cases, your lender may choose the order in which creditors are repaid first. In some cases, your lender may choose the order in which creditors are repaid. If not, prioritize paying off your highest-interest debt.

DEBT CONSOLIDATION AND CREDIT SCORES

In the long run, a consolidation loan may improve your credit score. Paying off the principal portion of the loan sooner can help keep interest payments low. This, in turn, can help raise your credit score, making you more likely to be approved for better rates by creditors.

However, rolling over existing loans into new ones may hurt your credit score at first. This is because credit scores favor debts with longer, more consistent payment histories. If you consolidate your credit card debt but keep using the credit cards you paid off, you risk increasing your overall debt load, which can harm your credit score.

Does Debt Consolidation Hurt Your Credit Score?

Debt consolidation may temporarily lower your credit score due to a credit inquiry, but if used correctly, it can improve your credit score in the long run. Most people who make their new payments on time see a significant increase in their credit score as they avoid missing payments and reduce their percentage of utilization.

EFFECTIVE DEBT CONSOLIDATION AND PAYMENT STRATEGY

The best method for debt consolidation and repayment will be determined by the amount owed, your ability to repay it, your credit score, and other factors specific to your financial situation. It is critical that you consolidate in such a way that you can make the new monthly payments and save money on monthly payments or overall interest.

1. FASTER DEBT REPAYMENT

Taking out a debt consolidation loan may help you get closer to total debt repayment, especially if you have significant credit card debt. Credit cards do not have a set timeline for paying off a balance, whereas a consolidation loan has fixed monthly payments with a distinct beginning and end dates

Takeaway: If you pay off your debt faster, you may end up paying less interest overall. Furthermore, the sooner you pay off your debt, the sooner you can start putting money toward other goals, such as an emergency or retirement fund.

2. SIMPLIFIED FINANCES

Because you only have one payment when you consolidate all of your debt, you no longer have to worry about multiple due dates each month. Furthermore, the payment is consistent month after month, so you know exactly how much money to set aside.

Takeaway: Because the loan funds are used to pay off other debts, debt consolidation can combine two or three payments into one. This can simplify budgeting and reduce the likelihood of missed payments.

3. LOWER INTEREST RATES

The average credit card rate is around 19.6 percent as of January 2023. Meanwhile, the average personal loan interest rate is slightly higher than 10.6 percent. Of course, rates vary depending on your credit score, loan amount, and term length, but a debt consolidation loan is likely to have a lower interest rate than your credit card.

Takeaway: Debt consolidation loans for consumers with good to excellent credit typically have interest rates that are significantly lower than the average credit card.

4. FIXED REPAYMENT SCHEDULE

If you use a personal loan to pay off your debt, you'll know exactly how much you'll have to pay each month and when you'll have to make your final payment. If you only pay the minimum on a high-interest credit card, it could take years to pay it off.

Takeaway: With a fixed repayment schedule, your payment and interest rate remain constant for the duration of the loan, and there are no surprises in your monthly debt payment.

5. BOOST CREDIT

While a debt consolidation loan may initially lower your credit score due to a hard credit inquiry, it will most likely improve your score over time. This is because making on-time payments will be easier. Because your payment history accounts for 35% of your credit score, paying a single monthly bill on time should significantly improve your score. Furthermore, if any of your old debt was from credit cards and you keep your cards open, you'll have a better credit utilization ratio as well as a stronger credit history.

The amount owed accounts for 30% of your credit score, with the length of your credit history accounting for 15%. If you close your cards after paying them off, these two categories may lower your score. Maintain them open to improving your credit score.

Takeaway: Debt consolidation can improve your credit score more than not consolidating. This is especially true if you make on-time loan payments, as payment history is the most important factor in calculating your credit score.

4 DRAWBACKS OF DEBT CONSOLIDATION

There are also some downsides to debt consolidation that you should consider before taking out a loan.

1. IT WON'T SOLVE FINANCIAL PROBLEMS ON ITS OWN

Debt consolidation does not guarantee that you will not go into debt again. If you have a history of living above your means, you may do so again once you are debt-free. Make a realistic budget for yourself and stick to it to avoid this. You should also start saving for an emergency fund that will allow you to avoid using credit cards in the event of a financial emergency.

Takeaway: Debt consolidation can assist you in repaying your debts, but it will not eliminate the financial habits that got you into trouble in the first place, such as overspending or failing to save money for emergencies. By laying the groundwork for better financial behavior, you can prevent further debt accumulation.

2. THERE MAY BE UP-FRONT COSTS

- Some debt consolidation loans come with fees. These may include:
- Annual fees.
- Balance transfer fees.
- Closing costs.
- Loan origination fees.

Before taking out a debt consolidation loan, inquire about any fees associated with late payments or paying off your loan early. These fees can range from hundreds to thousands of dollars, depending on your lender. While paying these fees may still be worthwhile, you should consider them when deciding whether debt consolidation is right for you.

Takeaway: When considering debt consolidation loans, do your research and read the fine print carefully to ensure you understand the full costs.

3. YOU MAY PAY A HIGHER RATE

Your debt consolidation loan may have a higher interest rate than what you are currently paying on your debts. This could occur for several reasons, including your current credit score. If it's on the low end, the risk of default is higher, and you'll probably have to pay more for credit. The loan amount and loan term are two other factors that may cause you to pay more in interest. Extending the term of your loan may reduce your monthly payment, but you may end up paying more interest in the long run. To find the best debt consolidation solution, balance your immediate needs with your long-term goals.

Takeaway: Consolidation does not always reduce the interest rate on your debt, particularly if your credit score is less than ideal.

4. MISSING PAYMENTS WILL SET YOU BACK EVEN FURTHER

If you miss one of your monthly loan payments, you will almost certainly be charged a late payment fee. Furthermore, some lenders will charge you a returned payment fee if a payment is returned due to insufficient funds. These fees can significantly raise your borrowing costs.

Furthermore, because lenders typically report late payments to credit bureaus after 30 days, your credit score can suffer significant damage. This may make it more difficult to qualify for future loans and obtain the best interest rate. Enroll in the lender's automatic payment program, if one is available, to reduce the likelihood of missing a payment.

Takeaway: Before you take out a debt consolidation loan, make sure you can afford the monthly payments. Failure to make a payment can result in late fees and a lower credit score.

HOW TO DECIDE IF YOU SHOULD CONSOLIDATE YOUR DEBT

The answer to this question is dependent on your situation. That being said, here are some scenarios in which you might be a good fit:

1. YOU HAVE A GOOD CREDIT SCORE:

If you have a credit score of at least 670, you will have a better chance of obtaining a lower interest rate than you currently have on your debt, which could save you money.

2. YOU PREFER FIXED PAYMENTS:

A debt consolidation loan may be right for you if you prefer a fixed interest rate, repayment term, and monthly payment.

3. YOU WANT ONE MONTHLY PAYMENT:

If you don't like keeping track of multiple payments, a debt consolidation loan may be a good option.

4. YOU CAN REPAY THE LOAN:

Finally, a debt consolidation loan will only benefit you if you can repay it. If you can't, you risk digging yourself into a deeper financial hole.

HOW TO GET A DEBT CONSOLIDATION LOAN

If you believe that obtaining a debt consolidation loan is the best option for you, take the following steps to obtain one:

1. REVIEW YOUR CREDIT REPORT AND SCORE:

Examine your credit score to see if you meet the minimum credit score requirement set by the lender. Get a free copy of your credit report from AnnualCreditReport.com and review it for errors. If you find any, file a dispute with the appropriate credit bureaus as soon as possible. A bureau's response time can be up to 30 days.

2. DETERMINE THE AMOUNT OF YOUR LOAN:

Add up all of the debts you want to consolidate to figure out how much money you'll need to borrow. Consider potential origination fees, which are deducted from the loan amount.

3. INVESTIGATE VARIOUS LENDERS:

Examine the websites of various online lenders to learn about eligibility requirements, loan terms, and fees. Also, see if your local bank or credit union offers debt consolidation loans.

4. OBTAIN PRE-QUALIFICATION:

When you prequalify, each lender will provide you with an estimate of your loan rate and terms. Typically, the lender will perform only a soft credit check for pre-qualification, which means your credit score will not be affected.

5. APPLY

Depending on the lender, you may apply for your debt consolidation loan online, in person, or over the phone. Personal information such as your name, date of birth, and income will be requested.

6. Accept funds.

If you are approved, your lender may deposit your funds as soon as the next business day. Use the money to pay off your existing debts. To avoid damage to your credit score, repay the debt consolidation loan as agreed.

IS DEBT CONSOLIDATION A GOOD IDEA?

Debt consolidation is usually a good idea for borrowers who have several high-interest loans. However, it may only be possible if your credit score has improved since applying for the original loans. If your credit score isn't high enough to qualify for a lower interest rate, consolidating your debts may not be a good idea. You should also reconsider debt consolidation if you haven't addressed the underlying issues that led to your current debts, such as overspending. Paying off multiple debts. Credit card debt consolidation is not an excuse to run up new balances, and it can lead to more serious financial problems down the road.

WHEN YOU SHOULD CONSOLIDATE YOUR DEBT

Debt consolidation can be a wise financial decision in the right circumstances, but it isn't always the best option. If you have:

- **A LARGE AMOUNT OF DEBT:**
  If you only have a small amount of debt that you can pay off in a year or less, debt consolidation is probably not worth the fees and credit checks that come with a new loan.

- **ADDITIONAL PLANS TO IMPROVE YOUR FINANCES:**
  While some debts, such as medical loans, are unavoidable, others are the result of excessive spending or other financially risky behavior. Before you consolidate your debt, examine your spending habits and devise a plan to get your finances under control. Otherwise, you risk accruing even more debt after debt consolidation.

- **A CREDIT SCORE HIGH ENOUGH TO QUALIFY FOR A LOWER INTEREST RATE:**
  If your credit score has improved since you took out your previous loans, you are more likely to qualify for a debt consolidation rate that is lower than your current rates. This can help you save money on interest over the loan's life.

- **CASH FLOW THAT COMFORTABLY COVERS MONTHLY DEBT SERVICE:**
  Only consolidate your debt if your income is sufficient to cover the new monthly payment. While consolidation may lower your overall monthly payment, it is not a good option if you are currently unable to cover your monthly debt service.

BUDGET AND FINANCIAL STABILITY

A budget contributes to financial stability. A budget makes it easier to pay bills on time, build an emergency fund, and save for major purchases like a car or home by tracking expenses and sticking to a plan. Overall, a budget puts a person on a better financial footing in the short and long term.

1. IT HELPS YOU KEEP YOUR EYE ON THE PRIZE

A budget assists you in determining and working toward long-term goals. How will you ever save enough money to buy a car or put a down payment on a house if you just drift aimlessly through life, tossing your money at every pretty, shiny object that happens to catch your eye? A budget forces you to set goals, save money, track your progress, and turn your dreams into reality. Okay, so it's painful to realize that the brand-new Xbox game or the gorgeous cashmere sweater in the store window is out of your price range. However, if you remind yourself that you're saving for a new house, it will be much easier to walk out of the store empty-handed.

2. IT HELPS ENSURE YOU DON'T SPEND MONEY YOU DON'T HAVE

Far too many consumers spend money they don't have, and we're all to blame. The average credit card debt per household will be $5,525 in 2021. People used to know whether they were living within their means before the age of plastic. At the end of the month, if they had enough money to pay their bills and save some, they were on track. People who overuse and abuse credit cards these days often don't realize they're overspending until they're drowning in debt.

However, if you create and follow a budget, you will never be in this precarious position. You'll know how much money you make, how much you can spend each month, and how much you need to save. Crunching numbers and keeping track of a budget isn't nearly as enjoyable as going on a shameless shopping spree. But consider this: when your spendthrift friends are visiting a debt counselor this time next year, you'll be on your way to that European vacation you've been saving for—or, better yet, moving into your new home.

3. IT HELPS LEAD TO A HAPPIER RETIREMENT

Assume you spend your money wisely, stick to your budget, and never have credit card debt. Excellent work! But aren't you leaving something out? As important as it is to spend your money wisely today, saving for the future is also a critical budget. If you set aside a portion of your monthly earnings to contribute to your IRA, 401(k), or other retirement funds, you'll eventually accumulate a sizable nest egg. Although you may have to make some sacrifices now, it will be well worth it in the long run. After all, would you rather spend your golden years golfing and going to the beach or working as a greeter at the local grocery store? Exactly

4. IT HELPS YOU PREPARE FOR EMERGENCIES

Life is full of surprises, some of which are better than others. When you are laid off, become ill or injured, divorce, or have a death in the family, it can cause serious financial problems. Of course, these emergencies always seem to strike at the worst possible time when you're already short on cash. This is precisely why everyone requires an emergency fund.

Your budget should include an emergency fund of three to six months' worth of living expenses. This extra cash will keep you from spiraling into debt following a life crisis. Of course, saving three to six months' worth of living expenses will take time.

Do not immediately deposit the majority of your paycheck into your emergency fund. Budget for it set realistic goals, and start small. Even if you only set aside $10 to $30 per week, your emergency fund will gradually grow. Depending on your approach, budgeting apps like Mint or YNAB provide tools for creating an emergency fund.

5. IT HELPS SHED LIGHT ON BAD SPENDING HABITS

Building a budget forces, you to examine your spending habits. You may notice that you are spending money on items that you do not require. Do you watch all 500 channels on your expensive extended cable package or multiple streaming subscriptions? Do you truly require 30 pairs of black shoes? Budgeting enables you to reconsider your spending habits and refocus on your financial objectives.

6. IT'S BETTER THAN COUNTING SHEEP

Maintaining a budget will also allow you to sleep better. How many nights have you tossed and turned worrying about how you were going to pay your bills? People who lose sleep over financial issues are allowing their money to control them. Regain control. You'll never have to worry about money again if you budget wisely. Of course, this is only the tip of the iceberg. There are numerous other benefits to sticking to a budget. So why wait? It's time to start budgeting!

IMPORTANCE OF MANAGING DEBT

Debt management is a method of controlling your debt through financial planning and budgeting. A debt management plan's goal is to use these strategies to help you reduce your current debt and eventually eliminate it.

STEPS TO MORE EFFECTIVELY MANAGE AND REDUCE YOUR DEBT:

You've already taken a step in the right direction if you're looking for a better way to manage your debt to eliminate most or all of it. As you prepare to move forward, keep in mind that some debt isn't bad a mortgage can help you achieve your goal of owning a home and may help you build wealth if the value of your home increases. However, having too much or the wrong kind of debt, such as high-interest credit card debt, can limit your ability to pursue other financial goals. Consider these seven steps to help you manage your debt more effectively.

1 TAKE ACCOUNT OF YOUR ACCOUNTS

First and foremost, make a list of all your current debts. Include the interest rate on each so you can see which ones are causing you the most financial hardship.

2. CHECK YOUR CREDIT REPORT

Request a free copy of your credit report. One or more of the three credit-reporting agencies opens in a new window. This will assist you in ensuring that you have not forgotten about an outstanding debt. Furthermore, it's always a good idea to check for unfamiliar accounts. If you want to know your credit score, contact your bank or credit card company to see if they can provide it to you for free.

3. LOOK FOR OPPORTUNITIES TO CONSOLIDATE

Can you combine multiple high-interest loans into a single loan with a lower interest rate? Are you able to obtain a low-interest personal loan to pay off high-interest credit card balances? Before consolidating or refinancing any student loans, carefully consider your eligibility for federal loan forgiveness programs that may be affected by loan consolidation or refinancing.

4. BE HONEST ABOUT YOUR SPENDING

If your debt is making you feel overwhelmed, it's time to take an honest look at what you're spending each month. Are there any expenses you can reduce or eliminate? Limiting the amount of new debt, you take on is an important part of debt reduction.

5. DETERMINE HOW MUCH YOU HAVE TO PAY

After you've consolidated, figure out how much you'll have to pay each month by noting the minimum payments and entering the total into your budget. If the amount is greater than you can afford, you may need to contact lenders to discuss different terms.

6. FIGURE OUT HOW MUCH EXTRA YOU CAN BUDGET

Determine how much extra money you can devote to debt reduction once you have a baseline of how much you have to pay each month in your budget. Hopefully, the expenses you cut will give you a little more money to put toward this goal.

7. DETERMINE YOUR DEBT-REDUCTION STRATEGY

It is completely up to you how you handle your debt. The two most popular strategies are to pay off the balances with the highest interest rates first or to pay off the balances with the lowest interest rates first. The former will save you more money in the long run, but the latter will assist you in maintaining momentum and seeing progress. In any case, you're moving in the right direction, so stick to your plan!

HOW TO ENCOURAGE PEOPLE IN DEBT

1. This is the experience you're having, not who you are.
2. Belief in yourself, and you'll get there.
3. You're doing fantastic!
4. This is difficult, but you are stronger.
5. Don't worry. You can do it!
6. Best wishes for today! I am confident in your abilities.
7. You're making a significant difference, and I'm so proud of you!
8. I'm sending you positive vibes and happy thoughts.
9. If I can't do great things, I can do small things well.
10. I understand that things are difficult right now, but I also know you have what it takes to get through them.
11. I'm Sending positive vibes your way I believe in you and do no doubt that you will succeed.
12. I'm keeping you in my thoughts, especially today.
13. Amid adversity, there is opportunity.
14. We have friends for both our happy and sad days. I hope you understand that I am still your friend.
15. I'm sorry you're going through this, but it'll be over soon.
16. You are constantly in my thoughts and my heart
17. Courage, dear heart
18. You are incredibly strong, and you are amazing for facing this with such bravery.
19. You know where to find me if you ever need to talk or just cry!
20. I wish you a better day today.
21. The next chapter of your life will be incredible.

www.ingramcontent.com/pod-product-compliance
Lightning Source LLC
Chambersburg PA
CBHW071124240526
45465CB00023B/809